More Praise for *Cormorant on the*

Gloria Monaghan's collection, *Cormo* gift, each section jettisoning us into new territory we must navigate with the deft hand of a confident poet. The poems are often in conversation with music, other writers, or movies, many as persona. Right from the starting poem, "Attic," the speaker is *deeply afraid* in the familiar. The poems that follow unveil places rife with sensory memory (*smell of well water and rust*), detail, and are peopled with specific inhabitants, real and imagined. There are threads of connection among the disparate sections: flora and fauna abound, Queen Anne's lace and the Rose of Sharon; cats and dogs and crickets and butterflies move through, and the obvious breadth of knowledge and curiosity of the poet. You finish this collection and want to read it again, but first maybe do some fun research into Oscar Wilde or Montgomery Clift and Elizabeth Taylor (Bessie.)
— **Sarah Dickenson Snyder**, author of *Now These Three Remain*

Cormorant on the Strand

Gloria Monaghan

Pat —
with so much
love - light

LILY POETRY REVIEW BOOKS

Library of Congress Control Number: 2023930411

Cover art: Frank Navin
Design and Layout: Michael d'Entremont McInnis

ISBN: 978-1-957755-16-8

Published by Lily Poetry Review Books
223 Winter Street
Whitman, MA 02382
https://lilypoetryreview.blog/

To my mother, Johanna Elizabeth Navin Monaghan

Contents

Sebastian Melmoth

The Sensible Thing

Monty Clift

Cormorant on the Strand

Swiss School

Attic

I am in a familiar house.
I call for justice, but the number is guilt.
Cavalier doors of past lives.
The old familiar attic,
the ancient wallpaper and sediment of rock
exposed, and I am deeply afraid.

Mariposa

Lost boy on the flyer;
I didn't get your name
riding by on my bike, in Provincetown,
but I know whoever took you
wanted something.
Too young and unaware to protect yourself,
but then a butterfly flew
straight into my face, young, also an adolescent.

Swiss School Song

Fourth grade in the back of the school in the fallen woods.
A Swiss school without walls,
I see my brothers asleep at their desks.

Sunlight through the apple leaves a happiness
playing on my face through branches
in and out of the shadow and light.

Songs pour out of me into the trees.
Below, boys on dirt bikes race and dive
gray-green weeds bent and dry
light dust over my Levi's,

and return to class without walls
with empty folders.

Golden Rod

(revoke: to call back)

Sometimes in my mind I go to the creek
it smells like clay and ferns line the banks.
Water striders jump from one lily pad to another.
We walk through tunnels.
Tennis shoes against the walls so we don't get wet
white and green mossed stones along the bottom of the creek.

Camille
fourteen years old, braids
neither boyish nor girlish
faithful and pure like gold light in a dream
small hands
you draw a line in the sand with your shoe
and let me cross.

The common showers are white-walled
a smell of well water and rust
the silence and the large empty space
and vast spiders in corners.

CYO Camp

Under low Michigan skies
I was the Leshy on the rocks of Lake Michigan, forming my song.
Not mermaid, underwater fish, Ann Miller

there on the sand shore, alone collecting sea glass
dancing among the black lichen rocks.
Old white cottage from despair
a house of romance
surrounded by pine in darkness.
Rough green blanket to cover my body on the bunk bed.

Port Huron

On the long sand shore of Lake Michigan
in the fat maple trees and thin pine
a song far off within the wood
water and wind.

A black-haired Leshy sings on the rocks
small stories under low clouds
her white arms sway
mermaid on a black rock
alone and free.

She dances on the sand
green barnacles cling to black
and the seaweed is lost memory.

Spatterdock Song

(From 1822–1883, Francis Buchanan White collected several different species during the Challenger Expedition. Water spiders, water striders, water bugs, pond skaters, and water skippers [or Jesus bugs] belong to the class of true bugs, the *Gerridae.*)

Near the small brown creek
water spiders jump from yellow water lilies,
their songs impossible to hear,

except for the slumbering bottom fish beneath
that interpret within dreams of mud and rust
moving to a slow rhythm current out of pipes,
whiskered and black, swimming beneath the quick
impermanent large-eyed diving bell silver spider
jumping from one green leaf to another.

By the edge of the water I follow your journey,
silent wish even through the culverts
eventually leaving, walking back up
to the cottage camp for girls
without windows, doors, or gates.

Dreaming of the buddy system in Port Huron and the shoreline,
water spiders jumping on the lily pads, creek dirt, fern,
with Camille in the tunnels that go between the creeks.

The sea glass glitters in the sand;
brown, green, white, and sometimes blue.
The rocks are mothers crying for their lost sons,
their hair fallen in the waves.

Maude

My Departing Blossoms

My departing blossoms
Obviate parade.
— Emily Dickinson

In the summer's dwindling light, I see
dew drops on the fat leaves of the low trees,
four o'clock sun capturing the beauty of the last pink roses
withering and refusing to leave the sturdy stalk
held immobile, righteous, and red-tipped,

while the others lie scattered in the dirt below.
Such dignity in the face of death.
The light falls in the side garden heavy, sad
violet and orange sky, a kind of power in the green leaves.
I have forgotten my sins and rise like the light

into the small wide drops left by the rain
of the previous day to sit unabsorbed on the fat leaf
within the perfect pool, a universe of stillness
shouldered by the strength, kept quiet by light
held up by the green, injured by no one.

Willow

I hid in the willow tree when we first came out from the east.
The long, thin branches were like the hair of some far-off
wood goddess, promising immortality in moss stones,
to live in the deep green of tomorrow and sink into the quiet.

I want to paint a circle within a square like da Vinci, live in a room
with a milk-glass lamp above an old tubular metal twin bed,
have a bathroom with blue and gray small-flowered wallpaper from
1960,
the lower half a painted putty color, and a low sunken tub.

To exist in a Fitzgerald summer in Antibes in 1920,
and speak with my grandmother's mother, Maude.
There could be wicker furniture on the porch, there could be long days
on the farm in Saginaw, and cucumber, onion, and sour cream.

Each house has its own significance and dream.

Each dream from somewhere else.

All houses condemned by spirits.

All hands have eternal pain.

The Field

Consider the lilies of the field, how they grow; they toil not, neither do they spin.
— Matthew 6:25-34.

Be open to mystery, not everything is in straight lines.
— Leonardo da Vinci

Stand with your feet apart, sway your arms,
twist back and forth, as if you were in a field.
Your mouth, a yellow sprouted dandelion.
Tall grass past your ankles whispers through you,
small white flowers of abundance shackle your heart
a green garden snake moves in the dirt,
like a question 'will you be sad tomorrow?'

Rolling down the hill, short straight hair and freckles in the sunlight,
dirt on the hands, summer shorts, no fighting in the field.
Maybe I held your hand, sang a song.
Skunk grass, poverty at lunch; *Dark Shadows* at four.
She finally arrives to retrieve us into place in the yellow Mustang,
from the field of loss and the field of nothing where everything hap-
pened.

Garage

It is planting time and still cold in the garden
where I left the cat leash and the clover.
There doesn't seem to be enough green,
or plants; we need more of those and more

rattan chairs unraveling beneath the tulip tree
cushionless, faded, and outlined in dark teal.

In the dark night when dreams come, I wake,
fingers clutched, going over the same routine
the one where I say, *OK, this is it,*
except somehow I get convinced to stay,
grab the small animal to my chest, whispering.

In the creases of Grandmother's faded cream davenport,
I find tiny skeleton keys in a small pigskin case
(still smelling faintly of men's cologne, or aftershave, light lime evening)
lapsing centuries, world wars, doors into lost rooms, or Chryslers.
What doors do they unlock, kept in the breast of a man's shirt pocket or vest?

But it is her voice in the garage, voice without voice,
petunias, dirt, peat moss, and geranium.
Please, God, help me plant.

Forsythia

The early spring memory of my father was when we were sent to buy milk.
We went instead to the Italian pastry shop.
He let me pick out tea cookies.
On the way he hoisted me up on his shoulders.
I felt very tall.

While we walked, with me sitting on his shoulders,
I was slightly afraid.
I wanted to hold on to something.
So I put my hands over his eyes.
In this gesture I blinded my father,
who continued to walk unheeded into the future,
forgetting why we were sent.

Tweed[1]

I remember almost nothing of my grandmother's language,
only the smell of Dentyne gum and Tweed perfume.

Her real scent was not in the house
but in the garage; peat moss, lighter fluid, dead grass,
heat, darkness, and warmth from cement walls in summer.
Tools of men long gone, used by her on the walls,
stacked flower pots and garden gloves.

Her hands smelled of tobacco and cinnamon.
I asked to use her perfume; *yes, but don't bathe in it.*
Not sweet, not soft; bergamot, geranium, a woody scent.

We took the wicker chairs from the TV room
outside to sit under the willow tree,
to talk about all her dead friends, Elsie Krug, the MacIntoshes,
and the convent at the Immaculate Heart of Mary in Monroe.

My hair long and auburn from her
rinsing it with red wine vinegar.

---

1 Tweed perfume was launched by Maryel Tweed in 1933.

1916, James Flewelling Shoots His Friend by the Explosion of a Gun

Word was received that James Flewelling of St. Martins died when his friend fired at a woodpecker, with a breech loading gun while in search of a lost cow.

The futility of two men sitting on a log.
Perhaps the light was fading,
fireflies were coming up and crickets starting in the milkweed.

Gnats rose from the rotting log. They were smoking,
and good enough friends for the one
to take the other's rifle and shoot at a small bird right above their heads.

Was it frivolous, or a joke,
was it impetuous cocksure bloodlust
to fire at the red crown of a bird?

(His small striped body, white and black,
and his fine beak must have lured James into movement.)
Instead it all backfired,

the explosion smashing his childhood friend's skull,
injuring his own twisted face –
wildly missing the immortal bird,
who flew away to another branch in the deep pine.

Flewelling. The very name is like a bird who flies and never dies,
but repeats his mistakes, a bell in sometime spring
where hidden violets lie under moss and myrtle.

Mamma Roma[2]

If you can believe in the eternal mother
you can believe that a woman can do anything,
if provoked enough.

In the opening scene Mamma Roma is called
to sing at the table. Pigs walk
among them, as well as children.

She sings about being free.
Her husband sings about sage, rage,
and saints of happiness.

She calls her son *a stick.*

Verdi in the background. Anna Magnani,
eternal arch of the eternal sun,
Dante's circle of mud and shit.

A woman, soft or loud, young or old,
is capable of anything.
So it was in the beginning
                    and so it shall be in the end.

Whispering love to her black hair,
whispering empty promises,
a hound in the stars;
Mamma Roma, between centuries.

---

2 *Mamma Roma*: a 1962 Italian drama written and directed by Pier Paolo Pasolini

Tell Me, Did You Find the Violin?

Cruxifiction

A woman in agony on her porch steps.

Her giant body supported on either side
by daughter and son
their faces reflect three types of suffering:

physical loss, refusal
to accept the faltering body,
heavy, obscene sinking into gravity.

Morning in July, on the corner of Chubbuck and 3A.

They carry her; son and daughter.
He holds up the rear of her enormous body.
She has the tit. Mother's arms flail out.
Crucifixion in still life.

Descending,

she screams as they flank her heft.
Sister has her by the front, brother by the haunch.
Her face a wild, silent scream.

A woman held up
by her son and daughter
on the porch steps of her house.

A woman at six in the morning in July
being taken to a hospital.
A small, dark, broken Honda Civic idles on the curb.

A woman in agony on her porch.
Splintering stairs reveal a life of suffering
in silence in front of the TV in a muumuu.
Summer pansies, yellow and pink, border the driveway.

Descension,

her life building to this moment of redemption.
The children guide her to the hospital of a graven image,
Mandarin King stop light.
It wasn't always like this.

Swallowtail

The blue butterfly emerges along the path in the dunes
low to the ground near Queen Anne's lace:
polyxenes, swallowtail
whatever name you call her,
she is like the dust on your ankle in the heat of July.

An early slipper moon, Venus
each one present in the other's view.
Years ago men wrote about the moon,
called her *Cynthia,* as if it were a woman so close to their heart
held in early autumn like the forever beat
of high summer when clothes fall away from the body
in some sort of sad departure.

An early green tiny worm made its way
into my home, and I opened the door and set it free.

September

Cricket in the low summer grass,
dark-eyed and mysterious.
I planted the darkened violet heather
next to the fence
to bloom again next summer
like the bright magenta along 180,
flickering in the golden light
of early autumn.

I dug a deep hole,
tore out the crabgrass and weeds
with bare hands and
the gray cat jumped in to help dig.
Put down two plants side by side,
they will spread and take up
space along the wooden planks,
happy and wide in the deep sun.
I bought two as companions.
Maybe they made a pact not to blossom,
to die next to the stockade fence in dignity together,
like the shell of a mussel, or the cup of a petal
from the tulip tree shedding light in September.

A Woman Under the Influence[3]

The difference between the moss color of the pond
and the dark green pine in October is negligible.

Someone decided the cat was dead and buried Jerome,
only to realize he was not really dead but disregarded.

The difference between inside and outside;
not to be winnowed into useless grain.

Doctor, aren't you going to give her a shot?
the mother screamed, craning her neck.

The difference between inside and outside,
the newspaper and the radio, and your face and my face.

In a rendition of *Swan Lake;* green backyard four o'clock sun,
dancing with the children, Mabel said, "Come on, die for Mr. Jensen,
kids."

The difference between the sludge of the River Rouge
and the brown slime on the rocks below is non-existent.

Nick's solution was to take the kids to the beach
in foul weather in the back of the pickup.

They did take her, and she did come back, but different;
Cassavetes knew women could go insane after so much indignity.

---

3 *A Woman Under the Influence*: a 1974 film directed by John Cassavetes

She put her head on his chest,
looked into his eyes when talking.
How was that a lie?

Tell Me, Did You Find the Violin?

They say the Stradivarius could play a man,
and a man should learn to play a violin without effort.
I tried, on the mussel-strewn beach,
to make a plan.

In the plan I was not deceived
and all the waves came gentle and slow,
like the smell in the dunes that catches you off guard;
pine in sand, juniper, something you cannot name
dust on your body reminding you of a younger summer
when you were taut and brown on your bike
with a boy's charm, and nothing could hold you,
and how your body responded then to heat and touch
on the nude beach near the dirt road
lined with Queen Anne's lace, fennel, and desire.

Sebastian Melmoth

Sebastian Melmoth

Look, the cat is crying;
a small tear sits in his left eye.
Winter brought three storms in 21 days.

There is a thin veil of snow settling on the car,
on the branch of the mulberry tree.
The street is slick, and the children have gone
on the bus to a school
they will eventually forget.

The Cat of Knowledge[4]

I

Like a cat on the windowsill,
I regret nothing.
First the kitchen sink broke,
lime scent on the careful corner
of the bed sheet.

The tulip tree opened to the heat of the noon sun,
small green cups, held the yellow heart
in each leaf a rotation of deep love
the light moving down through the vast leaves.
I regret not fixing things sooner.

II

Trop peu, trop tard.

The last bird was a cardinal. Male.
Why was he talking to the sparrow?
Not cute. What could they have in common anyway.
The fine, lean cardinal; the small, dull sparrow.
But the cardinal, he stayed.
All of this is lost on me.
He even followed the sparrow
to the edge of the curb.

---

4 The title of this poem and some of the paraphrases allude to the Prologue to Alexander Pushkin's poem "Ruslan and Ludmila" (1820).

III

Move to the right, a song groans,
exterior gnarled braids of the trunk.
I embrace the tulip tree and lie
under it in a hammock while it swings
to the right and left
(the cat walks around in ceaseless wonder).
I hear it moaning in the night,
and have felt the rough edges of the trunk
with my small hands.

Disavowed

That bird clamoring from
the holly bush to the pine

black-capped, mad, iridescent
in laughter,

what kind of fool leaves his nest
of protection and leaps to the North?

Then the rain came, first soft
barely noticeable, and then persistent,

too close, too close was the hour when I woke
to see my hand withered and closed like a parsnip.

The light of the moon or streetlight
on my face and my hair grown long.

Incompetent[5]

The road to heaven is winding
and empty grows every bed.

I called you the constant gardener.
Thin, agile, disrepaired, and ornery,
you worked in the gas station and then in my garden.

There is a way to heaven from down here
lilaced, placid, dirt road, dust,
perhaps some Queen Anne's lace.
There is a horse with his nostril wet,
his shadowed eye inviting,
some rain rising up off the stones too.

5 The phrase and empty grows every bed was taken from John Berryman's "Dream Song I," which was influenced by Berryman's scholarly study of William Shakespeare.

Disclaimer

Must have been late summer when you died
when the husks overtake the living green.
Mexican street full of strangers where you fell
to avoid New York, Central Park, daffodils, and the rain.

What moment was it when you fell, missing your footing,
blood flowing down the street in Juárez through the gutter,
small black flies in the day heat, children staring,
and eventually the hospital, where no one came to watch or hold your hand?
Was it then you remembered the dust
of the football field below the grass, the hunger of love,
or the small dollhouse you made once for your daughter?
Painting the floor until there was no space left to walk.

Après le Deluge

On the boat the water came in too fast for us,
everything went under:
kittens, flowers, bedding, clocks.

It was a small boat and the water was gray.
Too many people died of the sun,
and we wept, for there was no place to sleep.

Everything then evaporated. We lost what we lost,
and kept heaven in our hearts, and some were cruel returning
to civility. So we smoked Dunhills at the edge of the boat,

tobacco-sweet smoke curled about our hands and hair,
the sea a wild and golden thing to dream about,
the kitten lost, some things are better untold.

Argos

For all I knew the dog was in the street.
Stupidly, he left the yard.
The dog of my heart left for the day.
His eyes shone with sorrow.

The sweet pea, the lettuce unfolding,
the petunias changing color –
all of this the dog missed.

A box turtle in the road.
Blue butterflies took me
out of the dunes,
the way I held grief.

Old maligned black Lab
flies in the corner of the eye;
a kind of low interest
in the people on the beach.

The injustice of the heart,
the lack of joy, and landlocked
hypocrisy
fed the black dog.

Sprawling piece of seaweed
coiled around a rope attached
to a buoy no longer tethered

the black dog walks hopeless
and free; his head hangs.

I thought it better not to tell her
about the dog.

I changed movement then.

I moved on
to a dream on the linnet's wing
thin, caustic, blue-flowered.

August, Month of the Immaculate Heart of Mary

A single brown leaf fell slowly
from the tulip tree and a bee
sawed his way through the air
like a dream of tomorrow, tomorrow.

The young Rose of Sharon bloomed white in the ivy;
the inner raspberry heart was like the lips of a boy lover
who stole your heart when he was 19 and you were 22.
Wide open pale-pink petals loom
over the green and softly the head bows open
the yellow stamen of despair.

The Sensible Thing

A Series

Debased,
humiliate, belittle, die down, bring down.
Queers, twink, ivory towers, youth sports.

Defrocked,
removal, crows, ravens, grackle.

Disbarred,
away, sailors, ocean, time.

Disjointed,
separated, lovers, money, wings.

Devalued,
roses, older women, bowling pins.

The Roofers

The roofers discuss (between demands to each other for tools)
their lives, no wives mentioned, no children.

They listen to house music and one says
he loves Ptown, their bodies glisten in the sun.

Whitman's woman stays behind the curtain
to look at the young men. Each one different.

They have names for their tools.
"Do you have the black girl?"

Why is the tool a *black girl?*
Is it because she is necessary for them?

Kind voices, even amiable, the leaves mercifully
separate us, and my jagged rock wall keeps them away.

The Dancers

Love is like the lion's tooth
— William Butler Yeats, "Crazy Jane Grown Old Looks at the Dancers"

Love is like the lion's tooth on Saint Paddy's Day.
We have forgotten our God and now kneel;
it takes a great deal to get out of bed in the middle of March.

Love is like a lion's tooth in the secret branch of death.
Cut away the outer edge, but do not cut the cranes
because they hold the secrets of the source of the thing,

which is etched in the mind of the rose not formed
only the creeping green lined with winter brown moves upward
on a new branch toward impossible sun thoughts

of an imagined past now lost. Who can remember the last rose that
fell with twinged yellow at the edges of the red decayed bloom
that October day when the sun decided to leave us?

In midmorning, I wake and find the stalks that can be removed
easily from the side garden, wind sharp on the tip of the ear,
dried fennel sloping toward something moving in the dark earth.

Snowdrops cluster together like young dancers, bowed heads
knowing no better, young girls awkward grace white, green,
slight, yellow enough to be in the center of it all,

thank God for them. Those who come through the darkness
too beautiful to bear, for us to hold and weep with startled joy,
snowdrops, and crocus unexpected love at the breast of the mother.

Redemption

A lonely mew of the gull on the rocks
head down, wings hover
brown rocks emerge over dead low tide
small black pebbles, white broken shells abandoned.

I fell asleep on the sand.
I heard you call me,
the ocean in my ear
clear as day.
It was a pure wonderful feeling,
you calling me through the wind,
all the rubbish of the day swept away.

I was not a thief but a wild priest
looking through the hedges at illegitimate roses.
The wind came up fast in early September
I could feel the winter waiting, a dark thing
in the mulberry bush
(in the low grass near the vines).

The Rose of Sharon dropped her noonday blossoms,
now closed like promises taken back,
cloistered in the grass, do not look at them –
you'll shatter (into nothing).

The cat carried a sparrow in his mouth,
turned toward the door.
I thought about survival,
and whether love would come again.

Provincetown

Up toward the steeplechase near the rooftops,
A Monarch butterfly carries his lover in his legs.
She folds her wings quiet, a pale dusted blue
his scent mesmerizes her into bliss.
Is he going to bury her or love her?

She surrenders as he flies her away
from predators who may be watching.
It will take hours for him to pass his sperm to her.
Later, much later he will die, and she will live.

She will go in search of the milkweed
give birth in meadow.
As he carries her, she changes pallor, white-blue wings
above the zinnias, peonies, and dahlias into the blue-white sky.
They are going to a place none of us have been in their love dream.

Lost One

I

In the dream of Cyprus, we were searching for a school.
I climbed the wall, even though they told me no.

Once over, I went the wrong way.
Our guide showed me the way with his second son.
We slid down the dirt path, a bright red flower at the bottom of the hill.
I took this as a good sign, the school was just over the hill.

II

Get yourself a second son and call him *Felix,*
a king to replace the old one.
Make him clever and strong
make him see you so as to defend you.

So he can stand in for you and whisper your name,
an antidote in his father's ear.
The first son no longer sees you
or even hears you
or even speaks to you.

The Sensible Thing

It could have been Sunday or
merely because the tide was out and the shoreline
littered with rock and shells, and other people's footprints.

The sensible thing would be simply
to stop when I could to end what was good.

Tide had receded way out,
boats sat on the sand like dogs
at their dinner bowls.

The small, plaintive cry of a single tern,
invisible in the blue sky;
waves receded slowing in sand.

A sparrow purred as he flew away,
wings beating in furious time.
Two men walked by, arguing
it was morning
and the sky was blue and rose and orange.

Trumpet Vine

You are spectacular, and often
the hummingbird will come to you
in early summer and bury her small head
into your blossom
                                        and not every summer
do you bloom, even preferring
                                        closure to luxury,
cloistered in the garden
a bright creeping orange.

Man Driving Home

The last thing he saw was the shadow
of a hawk across the highway.

He had a fierce generosity
about the dawn,
this hawk.

There was nothing whimsical about it,
perhaps it doesn't matter – all this shuffling about,
only to discover the final flowering of the trumpet vine.

In the dusk two cats sat in the garden
side by side and perfectly content.
The cats of knowledge, songs, and tales.

Monty Clift

Monty and Bessie in Heaven

Tell me, Monty, what did you do on earth?

I spent it lounging in a fog of dreams waiting
on a movie set looking at suffering.

Well, I spent my time in the garden with my children,
and, oh yeah, I spent my time with five husbands.
But in the end it was the peonies, their bowed pink heads
drooping with rain under the Rose of Sharon.

OK, OK. Forget it, Bess.
Your mother, do you ever think about your mother?

No, but I think about my grandmother in her garden.
Gardening gloves, musty smell of metal in the garage.
A smell so seductive that I get caught in a trance.
Her side garden comprised of purple iris, lamb's ear,
silver sage, catmint, and Russian sage.
Along the aged red brick wall, she planted petunias;
in the early evening, I could smell their light
sticky-sweet fragrance lifting me.
I was seventeen and could have done anything.
She wore these soft gray leather gloves when gardening.
Why did we do it?

What.

Why did we live in the screen?
So others could see us, Monty?

No, because in the end
I was living with Lorenzo, playing
a broken-down cowboy longing for his mother.

Oh, yes. The mousetrap.

Oh, no. Chekhov
died from walking in thin-soled shoes
in the dead of winter tutoring children.
I mean, that is what he died of eventually.
Let it go, Bess.

You'll be my pickup –
It seems like we spent the best part of our time
saying goodbye.

If I could only tell you how much I love you.

Tell Mama,
Tell Mama all.

Cormorant on the Strand

The crew had code words for me when on set.
Bad was *Georgia.*
Very bad was *Florida.*
The worst was *Zanzibar.*
You have to wonder about Zanzibar
and what it entailed
beyond speech, beyond body, the word itself.

A region of Tanzania, black coast,
a central Swahili trading town.
An unsettled place, a possession of Portugal,
and notorious Arab slave trader
Tippu Tip, who traded ivory and clove,
died in Stone Town in 1905.
Can you imagine being named after gunfire?

Eventually free
and blended into obscurity
a mix of
Arab, Bantu, Persian, and Indian.

After each overthrow, it appeared
to be independent of any country
a land unto itself
a direct rule, as it were.

When I was Georgia,
it was a given that anything
could happen; a light overturned,
a fall brought on by a combination of
Nembutal, Seconal, candy bourbon juice
lewd-monkey-throwing-food-at-a-party kind of Georgia.

What does it mean to be Georgia?
To be good again,
like when you are young and brush your teeth
before going to Mass.

The sun goes down in three layers:
gray-blue, dusk
a line of fire-orange, followed by a trail of purple.
You have some time to think.

In Florida I was picking food out of a dumpster,
soliciting grocery boys.
I'd been knifed in Los Angeles.

(I knew then I'd been knifed.)

In a certain month of summer Florida
the water temperature may exceed the air.
Parasites develop near the shoreline;
be aware not to tread so close to the shoreline,
be caustic but supreme when dealing with candy boys,
note shadows after five. Don't play cards with Kevin
until you've had a few more.

When in Zanzibar, all bets are off.
I once walked on the roof
of my New York brownstone
at the edge when I was in Zanzibar.

Zanzibar with its turtles,
thieves, skeletons, blue
water, and vast sand.

Be in their flowing cups freshly rememb'red.
This story shall the good man teach his son....[6]

Lorenzo asked why.
Larry, why do women fall in love with men?
In the summer, halved mussel shells scatter the beach
blue-silver outlined purple.

Zanzibar is not a place;
it is a location of the mind.
Ungovernable country,
a place in the sun
outlawed wilderness of wolves and women
dancing in the desert in Fellini's *8½*
tranced-out women of Dionysus
all the more sexual in their decline;
of course, it is the pubescent boys who dance
with her—eyes rolling in and out of her
head into the earth, sky, divine.
We seek and we find the edges
of these places where things come together.

---

6 From William Shakespeare's Henry V, Act IV, Scene iii

Remnants of my Property

Hey, old man.

Hi.

I didn't know then he was recording our conversations.
Every day I called my brother until the last picture
Freud.

I really should have won the Academy Award
for that picture.

My brother worked for the CIA,
a kind of recordkeeper.

My lines in *The Heiress*
spell it out; *I'm not a mercenary.*

After the accident I had to navigate things
differently, use my face in ways I never realized
I could; my hands, my walk,
as if some wild thing caught hold of me from the
inside –

I could not let anyone see
what I knew about my body.
I'm not a mercenary.

In *Suddenly, Last Summer,* I come to heal
Catherine in the aftermath of Saint Sebastian,
poet, lover, destroyer, fraud. Instead I became him.

Some horrible things were said on that set.
Katharine Hepburn spit in the director's face.
She did that for me,

can you imagine?

You are beneath contempt.

I remember it well, being beneath contempt.

I'm not a mercenary; I have
remnants of my property.

Raintree County

She may have seen him for what he was –
artist, saint, deplorable, genius.
He may have seen her for the same;
beauty, drug-addled, violet-eyed.

She sat there doing her hair,
simple white tight-fitting sweater, black pants.

He, black suit, white loosened collar, loose black tie,
black spectacles at the edge of his nose.

Cautioning his Bessie, *there is something I need to remind you about,*
was she shushing him, or were they just talking or gossiping?

There was no advice he could really give her other than

be yourself.

I will be myself,
I will need to rewrite some of these lines.
I will need something more to respond to than this ...
You know what I mean, Bessie.

There are no staged photos
of open hands on his knees.

A Place in the Sun

The best picture of Monty and Elizabeth Taylor
was on the set of *A Place in the Sun.*
He is 30, she is 17
part of a black-and-white studio series.
Their bodies engrave each other.

His hand squeezes her bicep,
she is laughing.
He has a cigarette in his mouth
managing a dazzling smile,
broad tweed jacket open white collar;

born for the screen and high-resolution photos,
she looks directly at the camera,
he, away to some guy dragging equipment.
Her body relaxed, pops
above beyond,

his hand in his pocket.
He calls her Bessie the Cow
at the premiere. Later,

after the accident, she stays with him,
puts her salary down for him
to star next to her in *Reflections*
in a Golden Eye.

In this photo there is glamour, the adobe wall of the studio,
the fake street, or intended alley
a moment stopped in time
immortalized lines
of his cheek, white teeth, and cigarette.

He carries her upside down
over his shoulder,
her broad backside an autumn bell;
maybe it was a green A-framed skirt.
A saint in the street.

Judas in the waiting room.
There is always someone
who understands you without words
a glance, a smile, a tear,
who cradles your head in their hands
saves you from the wreckage.
It is what some call
a haven of mercy,
the body is a home for the soul
we return to broken and bruised, cracked and lovely.

Acknowledgments

Bangkok Biennial Cloud 9 Pavilion: excerpt from "A Place in the Sun"

First Literary Review East: "The Attic"

Lily Poetry Review: "1916 James Flewelling Shoots His Friend by the Explosion of a Gun," "Sebastian Melmoth" "Remnants of My Property," "A Place in the Sun," "Raintree County," "Cormorant on the Strand"

Nixes Mate: "Spadderdock Song," "Port Huron"

NPR Sunday Poetry Series "The Sensible Thing"

Poetry2Go: Republication of "Sebastian Melmoth"

I am so grateful for the long-term collaboration and support of Cindy Hochman. Thank you to my friends in poetry especially Eileen Cleary, Christine Jones and Michael McInnis for making this book possible. Marissa DeLisle and Matt Mullen of Open Doors Arts Center for their continued support of poetry.

Notes

"CYO Camp" – CYO Girls Camp and CYO Boys Camp are located just 6 miles apart on the Lake Huron Shoreline. CYO Camps, owned and operated by the Catholic Youth Organization of Detroit, an independent Catholic lay organization, which responds to the needs of the poor of all creeds and ethnic backgrounds since 1923.

"Port Huron" – Ann Miller, an American dancer, singer, and actress. She is best remembered for her work in the Classical Hollywood cinema musicals of the 1940s and 1950s.

"The Field" – *Dark Shadows* is an American Gothic soap opera that originally aired weekdays on the ABC television network, from June 27, 1966, to April 2, 1971. The show depicted the lives, loves, trials, and tribulations of the wealthy Collins family of Collinsport, Maine, where a number of supernatural occurrences take place.

"Tweed" – Tweed, by Lenthéric: launched in France in 1933. It was not introduced in America until 1935. Tweed was released under the name Risque Tout when exported to Europe and Central and South America.

"1916, James Flewelling Shoots His Friend by the Explosion of a Gun" – taken from an obituary.

"Mamma Roma" – Pier Paolo Pasolini was an Italian film director, poet, writer, and intellectual, who also distinguished himself as an actor, journalist, novelist, playwright, and political figure. He remains a controversial personality in Italy due to his blunt style and the focus of some of his works on taboo sexual matters. He was assassinated by the Italian Mafia for his sexual preferences. His death remains controversial, as he was publicly accused as a pimp for homosexual men.

About the Author

Gloria Monaghan is a Professor at Wentworth University. She has previously published five books of poetry. Her poems have appeared in *Alexandria Quarterly, NPR Poem-a-Day, Lily Poetry Review, Mom Egg Review, Quartet* and *River Heron* among others. She has been nominated twice for the Pushcart Prize, as well as the Massachusetts Book Award, and the Griffin Prize.

CPSIA information can be obtained
at www.ICGtesting.com
Printed in the USA
LVHW101541050223
738568LV00005B/20

9 781957 755168